JOHN HARBISON

FOR VIOLIN ALONE

Commissioned by
New York's 92nd Street Y,
Cal Performances at the University of California, Berkeley
and the University Music Society at the University of Michigan, Ann Arbor, MI
for Jennifer Koh

First performance: 15 January 2015
at the 92nd Street Y, New York, NY
Jennifer Koh, violin

duration circa 21 minutes

AMP 8323
First Printing: June 2018

ISBN: 978-1-5400-2837-2

Associated Music Publishers, Inc.

DISTRIBUTED BY
HAL•LEONARD®
www.halleonard.com
www.musicsalesclassical.com

Composer's Note

FOR VIOLIN ALONE is in seven sections as follows:

I. Ground. Over the changes of a pattern that originated in
the Mississippi Delta, becoming one of our country's
important contributions to musical langauge, six variations.

II. Dance 1. Two character types, Poised and Impatient,
answer each other in various ways, arriving at
agreement at the conclusion.

III. Air. Melody, uniterrupted.

IV. March. Harried, not voluntary.

V. Dance 2. The need to get outside, accept athletic challenge.

VI. Duet. Reflection, the dialogue within yourself, leading to:

VII. Epilogue. Elements, what is left over.

— John Harbison
March 2018

Information on John Harbison and his works is available on musicsalesclassical.com

FOR VIOLIN ALONE

I. Ground

John Harbison

3. Tempo, flambuoyant

4. Tempo, brash

II. Dance 1

III. Air

IV. March

V. Dance 2

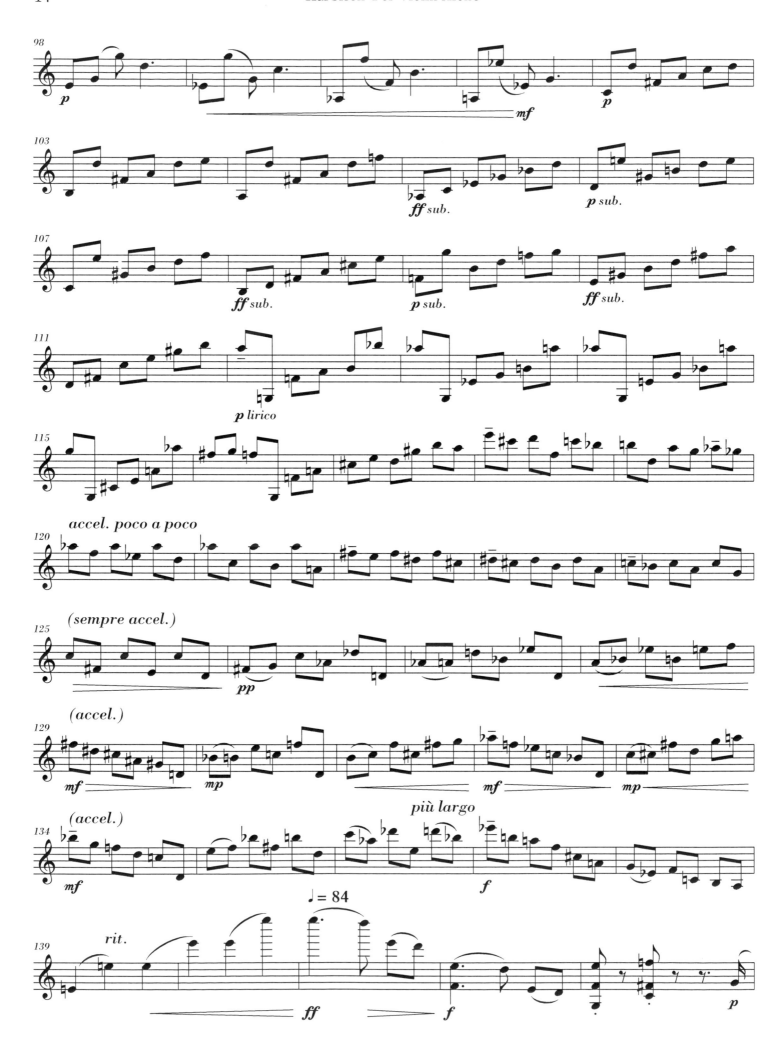

attacca

VI. Duet

Epilogue